W9-CIA-985

Spotlight on
ANCIENT CIVILIZATIONS
ROME

The Ancient Roman ECONOMY

Amelie von Zumbusch

Published in 2014 by The Rosen Publishing Group, Inc.
29 East 21st Street, New York, NY 10010

First Edition

Book Design: Kate Vlachos
Layout Design: Andrew Povolny

Photo Credits: Cover DEA Picture Library/De Agostini/Getty Images; pp. 4–5, 7, 9 (top), 12, 13, 14, 16, 18, DEA/A. Dagli Orti/De Agostini Picture Library/ Getty Images; pp. 6, 8 De Agostini Picture Library/Getty Images; p. 9 (bottom) Roman/The Bridgeman Art Library/Getty Images; pp. 10, 19 Danita Delimont/ Gallo Images/Getty Images; p. 11 Ariy/Shutterstock.com; p. 15 Jose Ignacio Soto/ Shutterstock.com; p. 17 Universal Images Group/Getty Images; p. 21 Mountainpix/ Shutterstock.com; p. 22 DEA/L. Pedicini/De Agostini Picture Library/Getty Images.

Library of Congress Cataloging-in-Publication Data

Zumbusch, Amelie von.
 The ancient Roman economy / by Amelie von Zumbusch. — First edition.
      p. cm. — (Spotlight on ancient civilizations: Rome)
 Includes index.
 ISBN 978-1-4777-0777-7 (library binding) — ISBN 978-1-4777-0887-3 (pbk.) — ISBN 978-1-4777-0888-0 (6-pack)
 1. Rome—Economic conditions—Juvenile literature. I. Title.
 HC39.Z86 2014
 330.937—dc23
                                      2013000209

Manufactured in the United States of America

CPSIA Compliance Information: Batch #S13PK2: For Further Information contact Rosen Publishing, New York, New York at 1-800-237-9932

CONTENTS

Work in Ancient Rome

Ancient Rome built up one of the most powerful civilizations in history. It was able to grow so powerful because of its strong economy. A country's economy is the way in which it organizes its **resources**, goods, and services.

This Roman relief, or carving, shows people doing some of the kinds of work that made the Roman economy run.

Ancient Roman society was made up of three main classes. The patricians were the richest class, made up of Rome's oldest families. The plebeians made up Rome's working class. They included farmers, craftsmen, merchants, and more. Patricians and plebeians were **citizens**, but Rome's many slaves were not. Slaves often came from places the Romans had **conquered**. They did many jobs for their masters.

Rome's Vast Empire

Roman civilization started in the city of Rome, in what is now Italy. From the beginning, though, the Romans fought with neighboring peoples and won control over their lands. Over time, the Romans came to control more and more land. At one point, a quarter of Earth's people were under Roman rule.

Workers unload a boat in this mosaic from the Roman city of Hadrumetum, in what is now Tunisia. A mosaic is a picture made from bits of tile or stone.

This statue of a wine ship came from the Roman settlement of Noviomagus Trevirorum, in what is now Germany. It likely honored a wine merchant who had died.

The Romans depended on the lands they conquered for resources, goods, and services. For example, they **imported,** or brought, tin from Britain. Egypt was a major source of grain. Greek slaves often worked as doctors or teachers. Rome's good road system and many ships made all this possible.

Growing Food

Farming was the backbone of Rome's economy. The patricians owned much of the land. They had big farms on which slaves did most of the work. They also hired plebeians or rented land to them in exchange for part of the **harvest**. Some plebeians owned small farms. However, many had to sell their land because they could not afford to farm it or were called away to fight in wars.

This Roman mosaic of a farm is from what is now Tunisia. That part of northern Africa provided the Romans with crops, such as wheat and grapes.

Northern Africa's rich farmland made it one of the richest parts of the Roman Empire.

The Romans raised many crops. Grains were the most important, followed by grapes and olives. Wine was made from grapes. Olives were pressed into olive oil for eating, cooking, and burning in lamps.

The Romans used oxen and mules to help them do heavy farmwork, such as plowing.

9

Making Food

The main grain that the Romans ate was wheat. Early on, it came from the countryside around Rome. In later years, Egypt, Sicily, and Tunisia supplied much of the empire's wheat. The Romans sometimes boiled wheat to make **porridge**. They made bread with wheat that had been ground into flour. Slaves ground flour with hand mills. Animals, such as donkeys, powered larger mills. In some places, water mills were used.

This painting from Ostia shows grain being unloaded from a boat. Ostia was Rome's port. Goods headed for Rome were shipped there. It had many grain storage containers.

Here, you can see the remains of ovens in a bakery in the Roman town of Pompeii, in Italy. Pompeii had more than 30 bakeries.

While some Romans baked their own bread at home, many bought bread from bakeries. Bakeries had huge, wood-burning ovens made of bricks covered in plaster. Many had their own mills.

Markets and Shops

Most Roman towns had several bakeries. There were many shops that sold other foods and wine, too. Barbers, lamp makers, jewelers, florists, and many other businesses had shops as well. Streets were lined with these shops, many of which had shutters that opened to the street. The shops were often on the ground floor of big apartment blocks called *insulae*.

This relief shows a Roman money changer's shop. Money changers changed coins of one land for those of another. They also held sums of money for people, as banks do today.

Cobblers are people who make shoes. This Roman relief shows a cobbler at work.

Towns also had markets, known as forums. These had many shops as well as temples and other important public buildings. Rome had several forums. The Forum Piscarium was a fish market, while the Forum Boarium began as a cattle market.

Building the Empire

As their empire grew, the Romans built new towns in the **provinces** they ruled. They also kept building new buildings in Rome itself. Construction was a key part of the Roman economy.

This relief shows Roman stonecutters at work. Some workers cut stone out of the ground, while others shaped stone or placed it during building.

Roman construction was very solid. Many of the things the Romans built still stand today. One example is the bridge of the Aqueduct of Segovia, in Spain.

Stone was an important building material. Workers, including slaves, cut it out of the ground in **quarries**. The Romans also used brick and tile in their buildings. These were made from clay and fired in special ovens called **kilns**. Concrete was another key building material. The Romans made very strong concrete by mixing rocks or broken brick with water, quicklime, and volcanic ash.

Mines and Metalworking

The Romans set up mines across the lands they ruled. They dug up the metals they needed to make the tools and weapons they used to build and defend their empire. Mines in Spain produced much gold and silver. Britain was a key source of tin, lead, and other metals. Some mines were tunnels dug deep into the ground, while in other spots the Romans dug up metals on the surface.

Blacksmiths make things from iron and steel. This Roman relief shows blacksmiths in their workshop. They used tools such as anvils, tongs, hammers, and pliers.

Roman soldiers used this mask during training. It is made of bronze, which is a mix of copper and tin.

Workers made many useful things from these metals, such as water pipes, cooking vessels, nails, and fishhooks. They also made the daggers, swords, and spears that Roman soldiers used.

Coins and Taxes

The Romans made coins from metal. The *as* was a small Roman coin made out of copper or bronze. The more valuable *denarius* was silver. The gold *aureus* was more valuable still.

Tax collectors, like the seated man shown here, bid on the right to collect taxes from a province. They paid the money up front and kept any extra money after the taxes were collected.

This Roman coin has a picture of the emperor Domitian on it. During the years that emperors ruled Rome, Roman coins often showed the current emperor.

The Romans taxed many things, such as mines, shipping goods through harbors, and grazing animals on public land. Some people paid their taxes with coins and others in grain. Government officials passed out this grain to the poor. At times, much of Rome's **population** depended on this grain to have enough to eat. The Roman government sometimes hired people to collect taxes in the provinces. This became a big money-making business.

Roman Women

Roman women had fewer rights than Roman men. They were expected to become wives and run their husbands' households. In early years, husbands had full power over their wives and controlled their **property**. Later, women often remained under their fathers' authority after marriage. This meant they could control their own property, giving them more economic freedom. Some Roman women even ran their own businesses.

Female slaves had to do whatever their owners said. Many worked as nurses, maids, or salespeople in shops. Their children became slaves, too. However, the children of freedwomen, or female slaves who had been set free, became citizens.

This mosaic shows a woman harvesting grapes. Female slaves often worked on farms, including vineyards. A vineyard is a farm for growing grapes.

Big Empire, Strong Economy

Rome's vast empire let its economy prosper. It provided the Romans with things that central Italy could not supply. Historians even think that the Romans conquered certain places just to control their resources. The trade **networks** that grew up between different parts of the empire added to Rome's wealth, too.

However, Rome's strong economy also fueled the empire's growth. Taxes paid for the powerful army that built and ruled the empire. Today, we can see that the growth of Rome's economy and empire were linked.

The big range of shops and goods in Roman towns was a sign of the strength of the Roman economy. This relief was a sign from a Roman coppersmith's shop.

GLOSSARY

citizens (SIH-tih-zenz) People who live in a country or other community and have certain rights

conquered (KON-kerd) Overcame something.

harvest (HAR-vist) A season's gathered crops.

imported (im-POR-ted) Brought from another country for sale or use.

kilns (KILNS) Ovens used to burn, bake, or dry things.

networks (NET-wurks) Systems or groups of things that connect to each other.

population (pop-yoo-LAY-shun) A group of animals or people living in the same place.

porridge (POR-ij) Grain boiled with water until thick and soft, like oatmeal.

property (PRO-per-tee) Things a person owns.

provinces (PRAH-vins-ez) Countries that are run by other countries.

quarries (KWOR-eez) Large holes, dug in the ground, from which stones are taken.

resources (REE-sawrs-ez) Supplies, sources of energy, or useful things.

INDEX

WEBSITES

Due to the changing nature of Internet links, PowerKids Press has developed an online list of websites related to the subject of this book. This site is updated regularly. Please use this link to access the list:
www.powerkidslinks.com/sacr/econ/